THE PHILLIP KEVEREN SERIES — EASY PIANO

EARLY ROCK 'N'

T0058901

— PIANO LEVEL —
EARLY INTERMEDIATE

ISBN 978-0-634-07358-8

HAL•LEONARD®
CORPORATION

7777 W. BLUEMOUND RD. P.O. BOX 13819 MILWAUKEE, WI 53213

Visit Hal Leonard Online at
www.halleonard.com

Visit Phillip at
www.phillipkeveren.com

PREFACE

"Rock Around the Clock" is often considered to be one of the songs that kicked off the rock 'n' roll era in 1955. All of the songs in this collection are from the 1950s and 1960s, gems from the early days of rock 'n' roll. Looking at these tunes from the vantage point of the early 21st century, they seem positively innocent. Naïve, even. The lyrics deal with love and life in a playful light. The melodies are tuneful and direct. The harmonies are straightforward and reassuring.

I believe these songs will continue to entertain for many generations to come. The Beach Boys are still the favored accompaniment for our family road trips—at the request of my teenagers! Pretty amazing, considering these songs were pop hits decades before they were even born.

So, rock around the clock!

Phillip Keveren

BIOGRAPHY

Phillip Keveren, a multi-talented keyboard artist and composer, has composed original works in a variety of genres from piano solo to symphonic orchestra. Mr. Keveren gives frequent concerts and workshops for teachers and their students in the United States, Canada, Europe, and Asia. Mr. Keveren holds a B.M. in composition from California State University Northridge and a M.M. in composition from the University of Southern California.

CONTENTS

ALL I HAVE TO DO IS DREAM

Words and Music by
BOUDLEAUX BRYANT
Arranged by Phillip Keveren

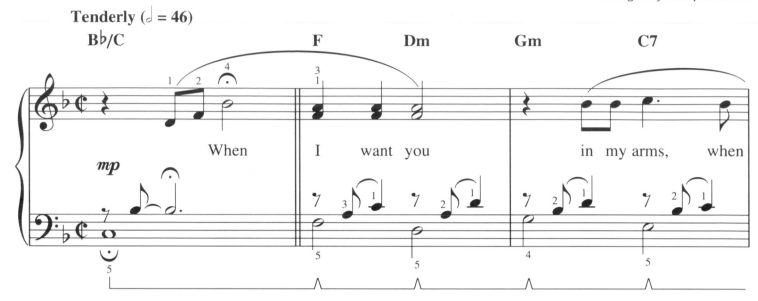

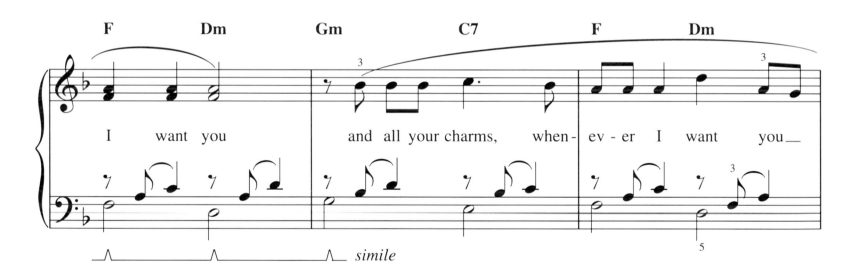

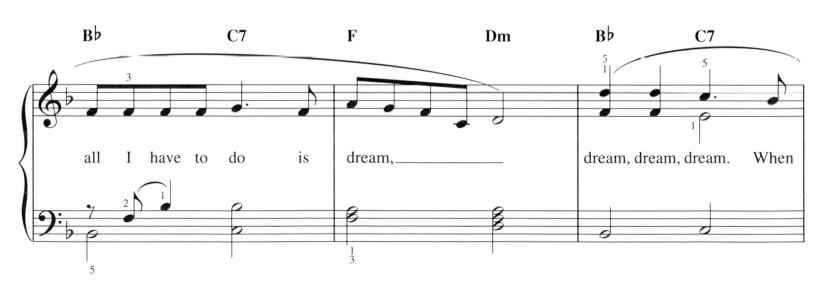

BLUE SUEDE SHOES

Words and Music by
CARL LEE PERKINS
Arranged by Phillip Keveren

Well, it's one for the mon-ey, two for the show,

three to get read-y, now go, cat, go! But don't you

step on my blue suede shoes. You can

do an-y-thing __ but lay off of my blue suede

shoes.

Well, you can

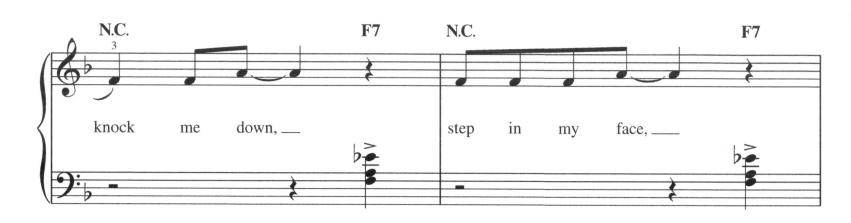

knock me down, ___

step in my face, ___

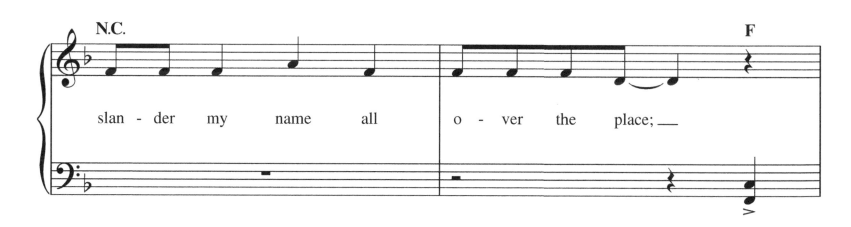

slan - der my name all

o - ver the place; ___

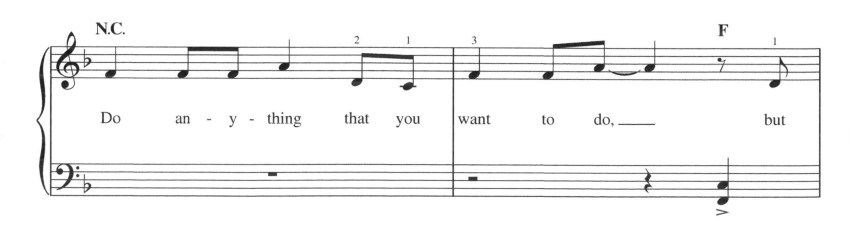

Do an - y - thing that you

want to do, _____ but

uh - uh, hon - ey, lay off of my shoes. _ Don't you

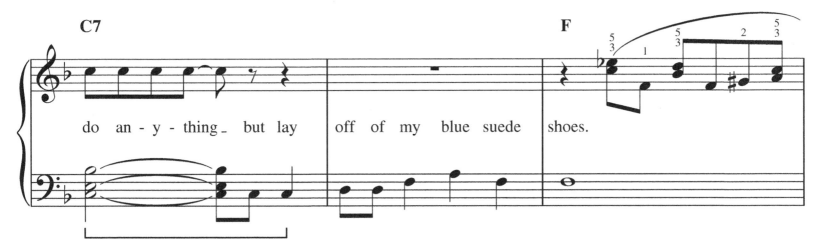

step on my blue suede shoes. You can

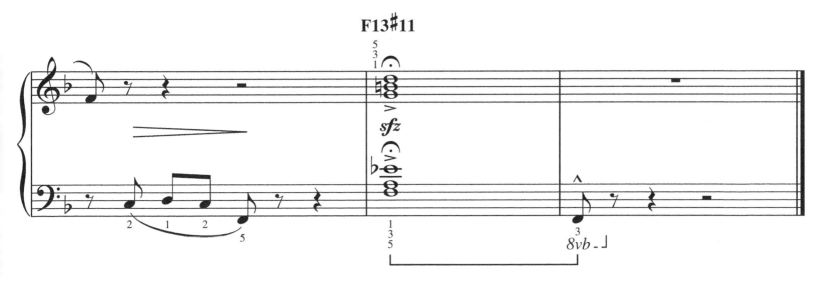

do an - y - thing _ but lay off of my blue suede shoes.

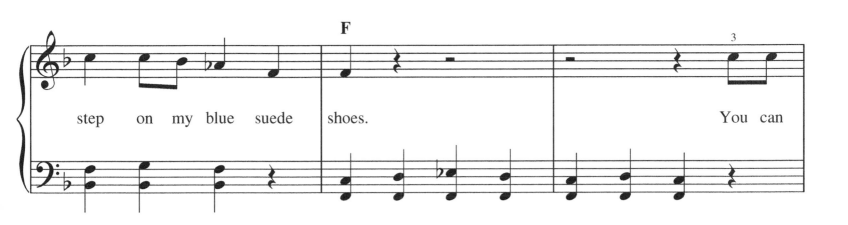

AT THE HOP

Words and Music by ARTHUR SINGER,
JOHN MADARA and DAVID WHITE
Arranged by Phillip Keveren

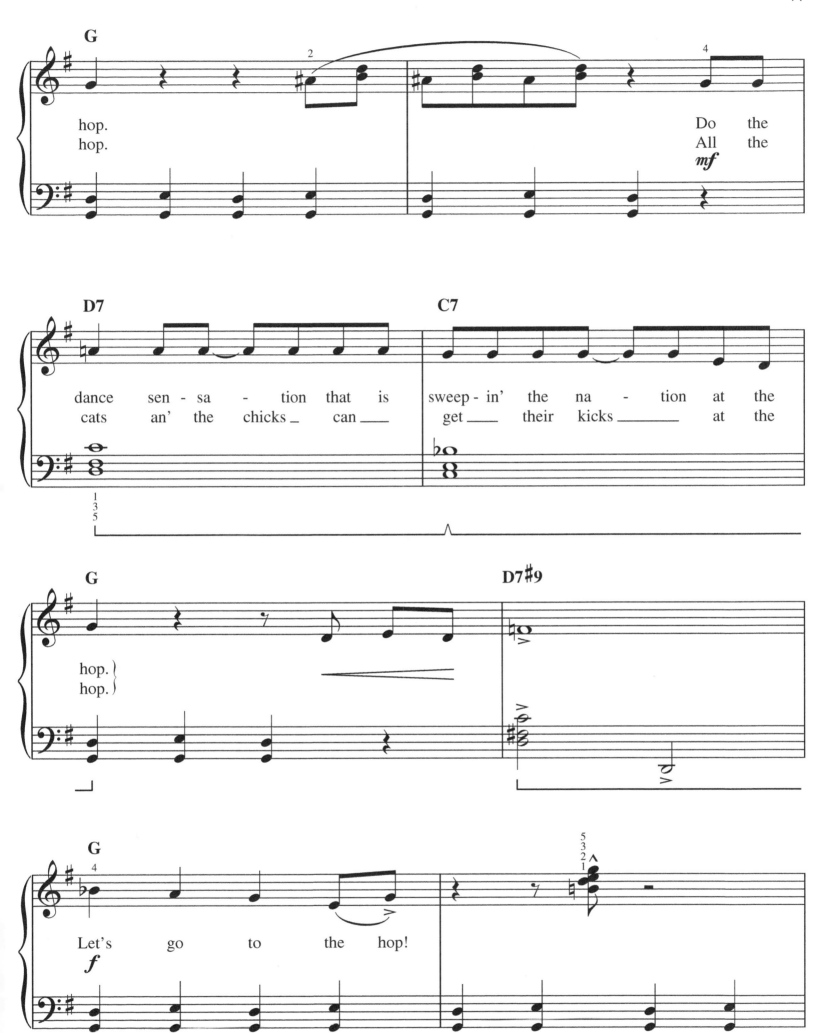

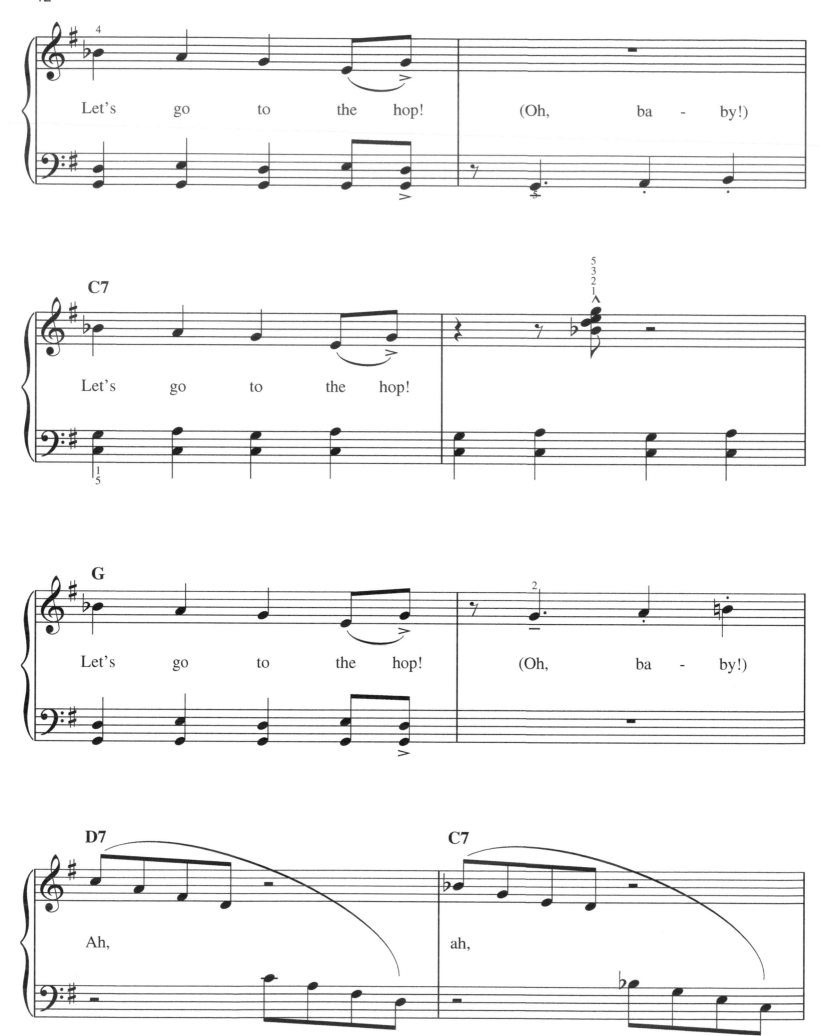

CALENDAR GIRL

Words and Music by HOWARD GREENFIELD
and NEIL SEDAKA
Arranged by Phillip Keveren

CRYING

Words and Music by ROY ORBISON
and JOE MELSON
Arranged by Phillip Keveren

Slowly, with longing

1. I was al - right for a
2. *(See additional lyrics)*

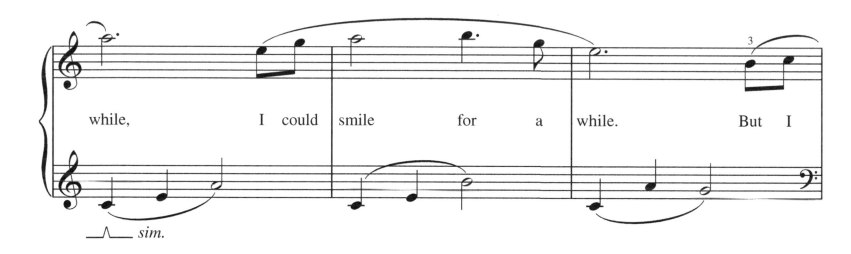

while,   I could smile   for a   while.   But I

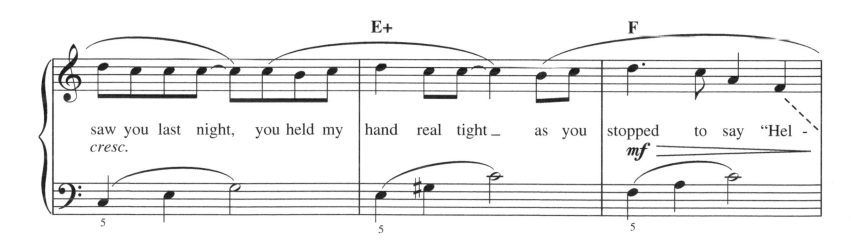

saw you last night,   you held my   hand real tight _ as you   stopped to say "Hel -

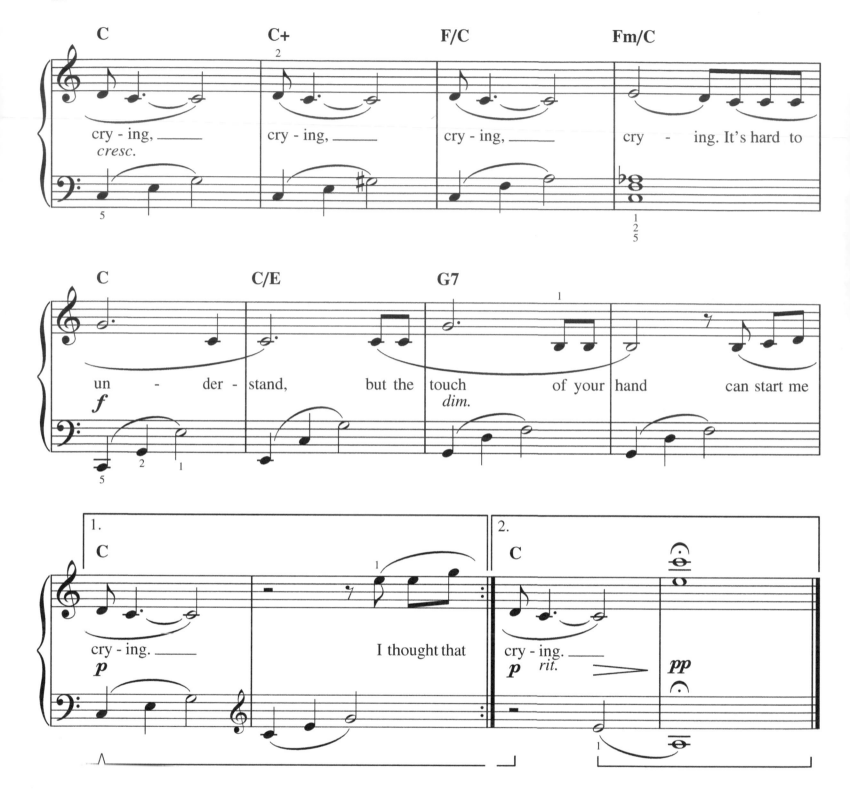

Additional Lyrics

2. I thought that I was over you
   But it's true, so true
   I love you even more than I did before.
   But darling, what can I do?
   For you don't love me and I'll always be
   Crying over you, crying over you.
   Yes, now you're gone and from this moment on
   I'll be crying, crying, crying, crying
   Yeah, crying, crying over you.

EARTH ANGEL

Words and Music by
JESSE BELVIN
Arranged by Phillip Keveren

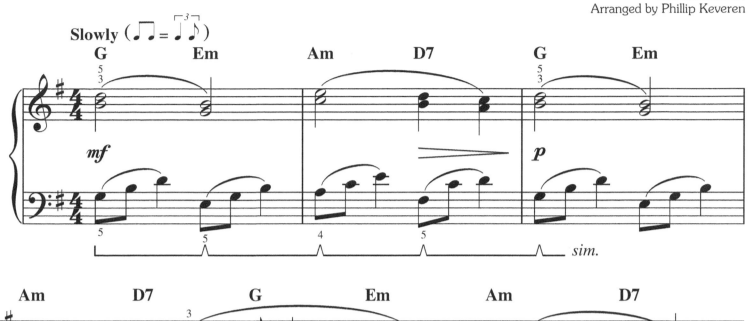

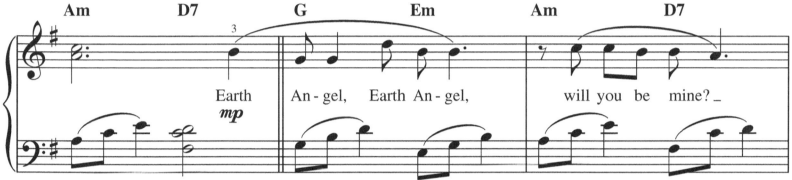

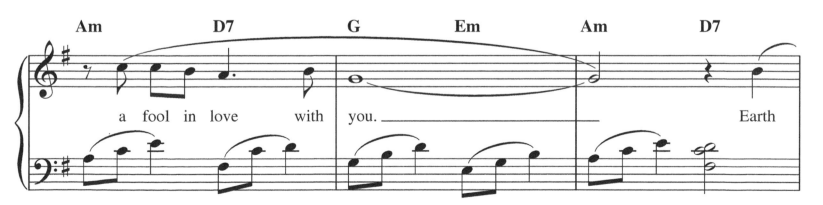

JOHNNY ANGEL

Words by LYNN DUDDY
Music by LEE POCKRISS
Arranged by Phillip Keveren

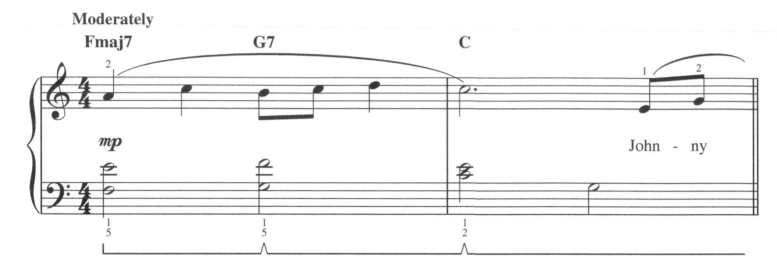

THE END OF THE WORLD

Words by SYLVIA DEE
Music by ARTHUR KENT
Arranged by Phillip Keveren

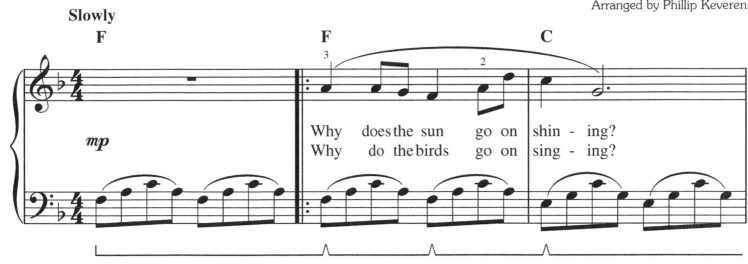

end-ed when I lost your love. I wake up in the morn ing and I

won - der why ev - 'ry - thing's the same as it

was. I can't un - der stand, no I can't un - der stand how

life goes on the way it does!

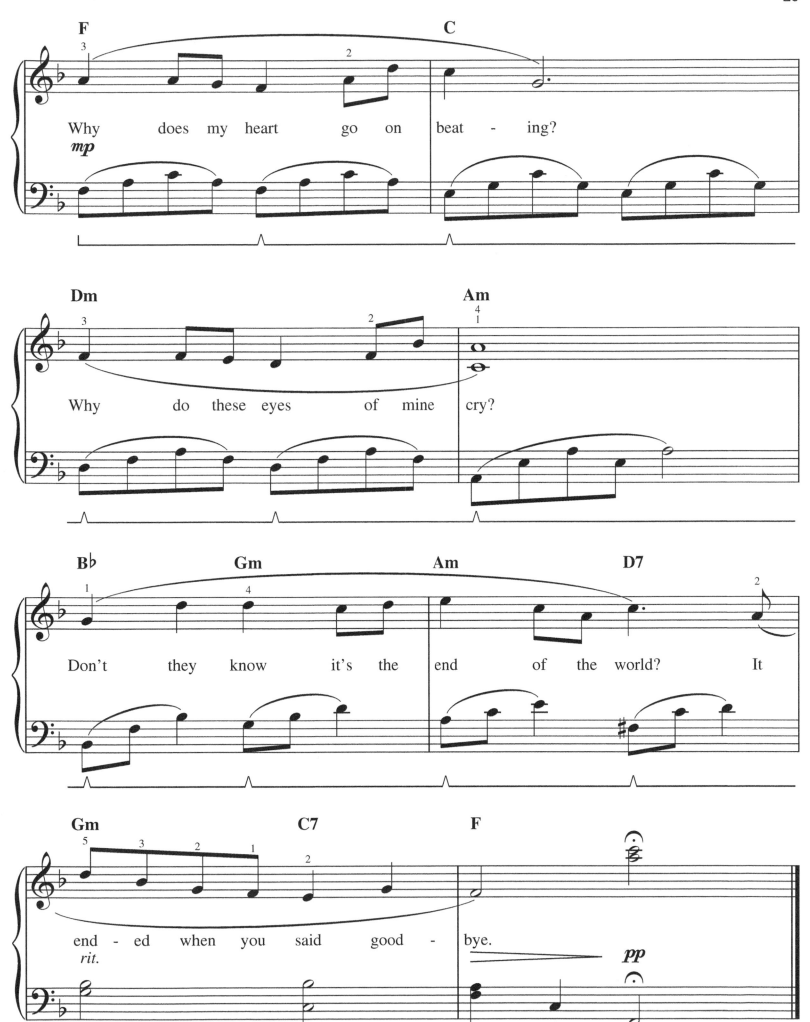

FUN, FUN, FUN

Words and Music by BRIAN WILSON
and MIKE LOVE
Arranged by Phillip Keveren

MOMENTS TO REMEMBER

Words by AL STILLMAN
Music by ROBERT ALLEN
Arranged by Phillip Keveren

Slowly, expressively (♩ = 92)

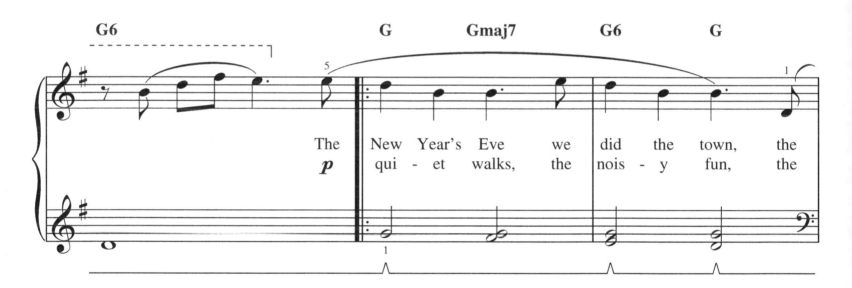

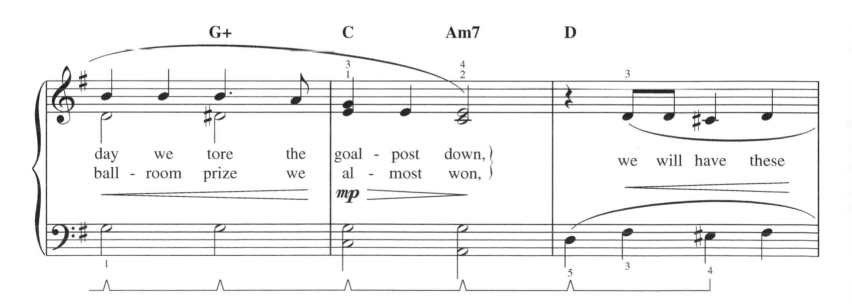

36

OH, PRETTY WOMAN

Words and Music by ROY ORBISON
and BILL DEES
Arranged by Phillip Keveren

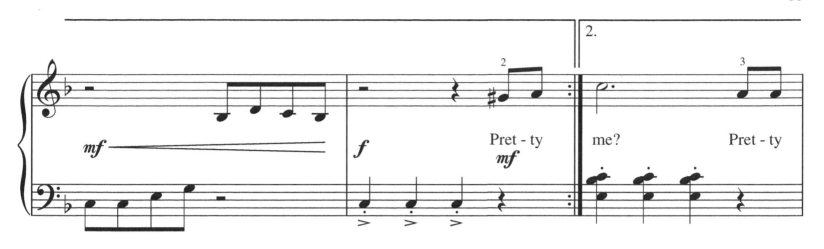

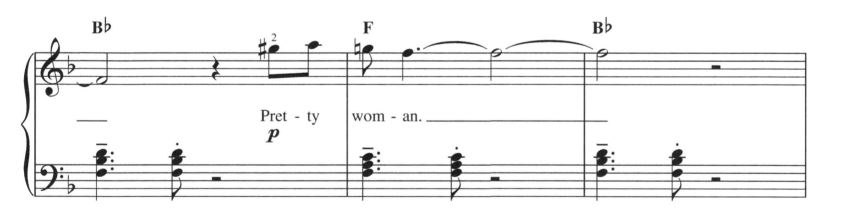

MY GUY

Words and Music by
WILLIAM "SMOKEY" ROBINSON
Arranged by Phillip Keveren

With a bounce

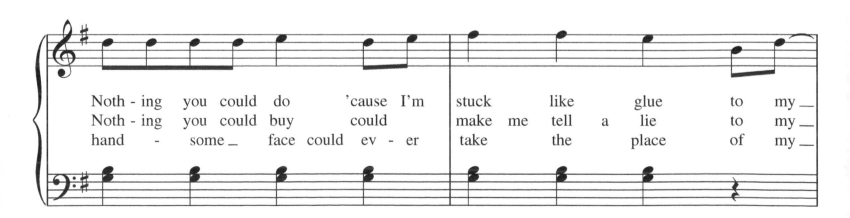

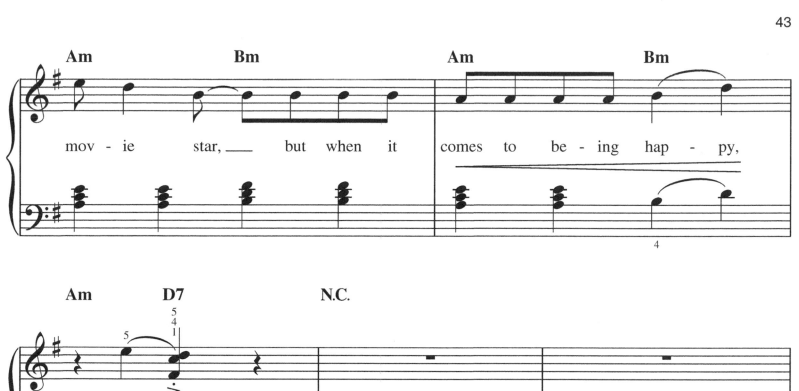

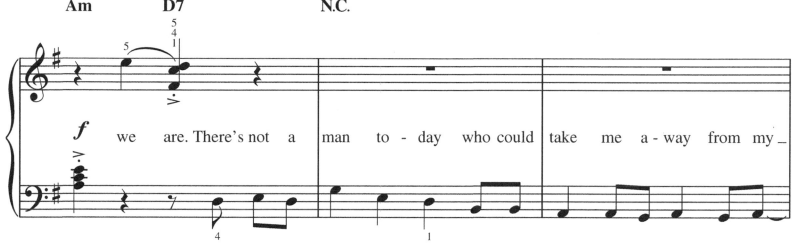

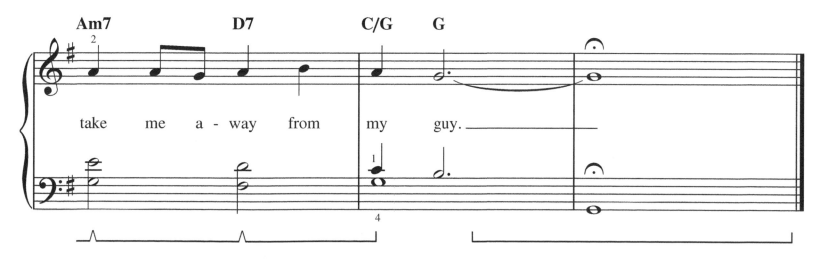

ONLY YOU
(And You Alone)

Words and Music by BUCK RAM
and ANDE RAND
Arranged by Phillip Keveren

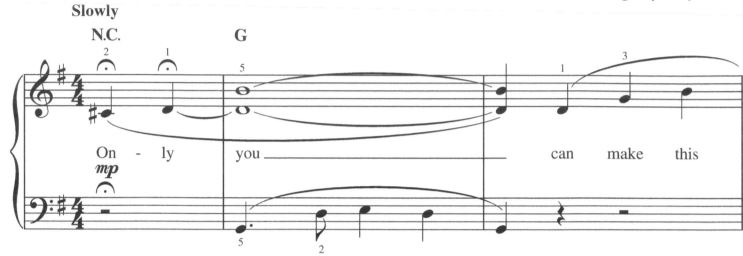

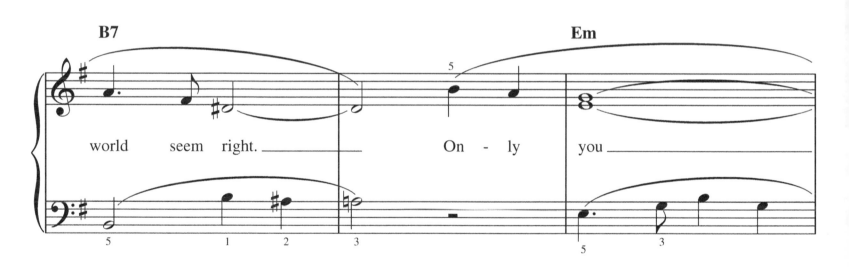

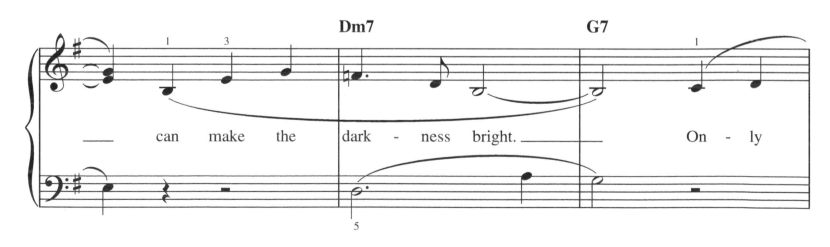

45

ROCK AROUND THE CLOCK

Words and Music by MAX C. FREEDMAN
and JIMMY DeKNIGHT
Arranged by Phillip Keveren

Medium Rock 'n' Roll

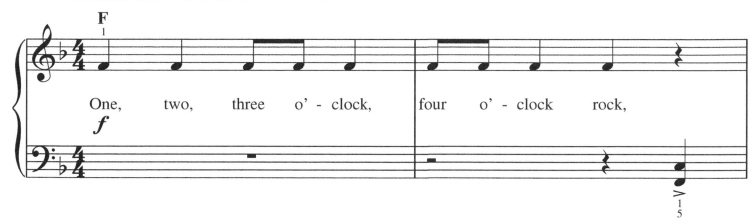

One, two, three o'-clock, four o'-clock rock,

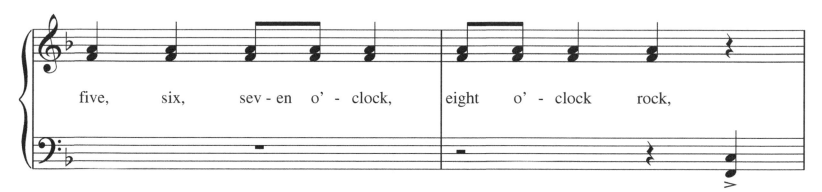

five, six, sev-en o'-clock, eight o'-clock rock,

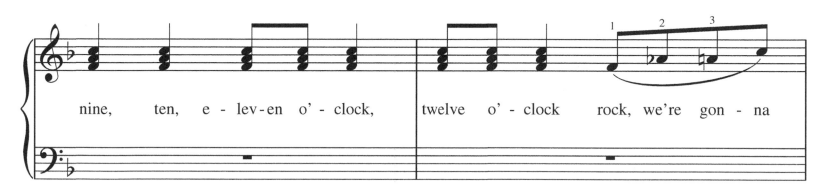

nine, ten, e-lev-en o'-clock, twelve o'-clock rock, we're gon-na

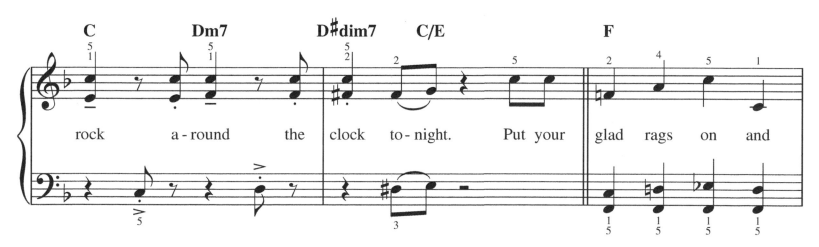

rock a-round the clock to-night. Put your glad rags on and

join me, Hon, __ we'll have some fun when the clock strikes one, __ we're gon - na

rock a - round the clock to - night, __ we're gon - na rock, rock, rock, 'til

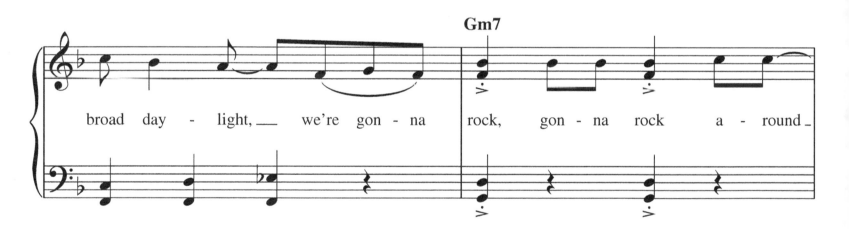

broad day - light, __ we're gon - na rock, gon - na rock a - round __

__ the clock __ to - night. __ When the

SPLISH SPLASH

Words and Music by BOBBY DARIN
and MURRAY KAUFMAN
Arranged by Phillip Keveren

Driving Rock

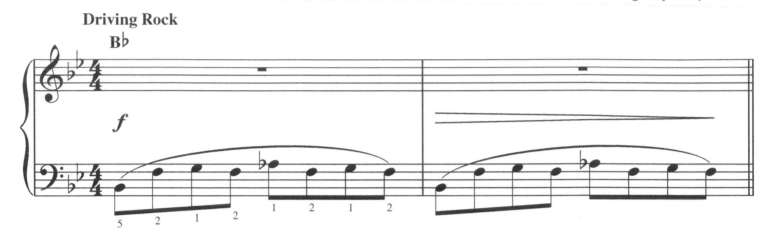

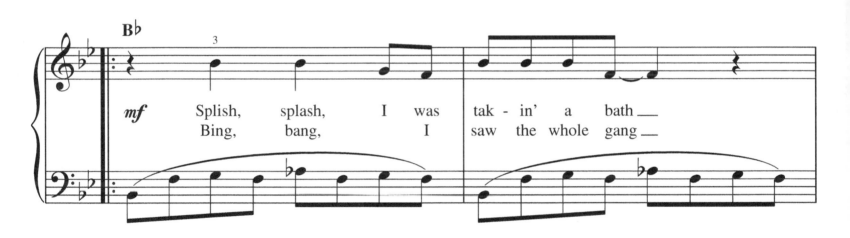

Splish, splash, I was tak-in' a bath __
Bing, bang, I saw the whole gang __

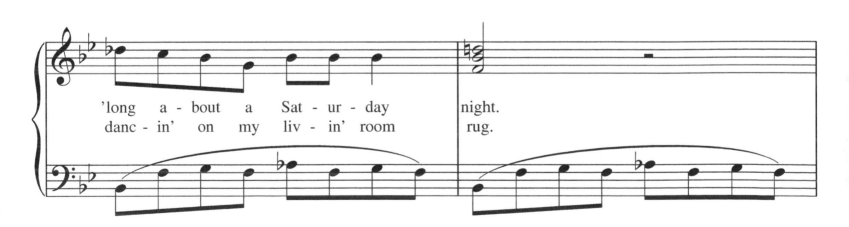

'long a-bout a Sat-ur-day night.
danc-in' on my liv-in' room rug.

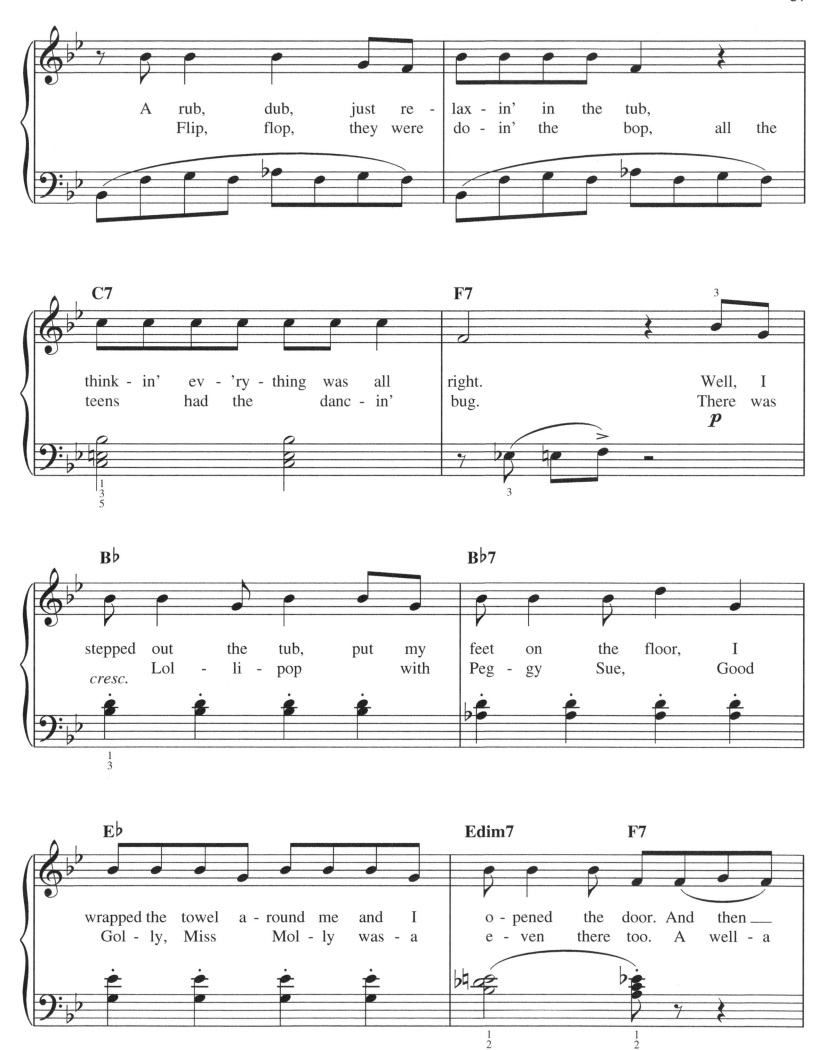

SURFIN' U.S.A.

Words and Music by
CHUCK BERRY
Arranged by Phillip Keveren

Solid Rock

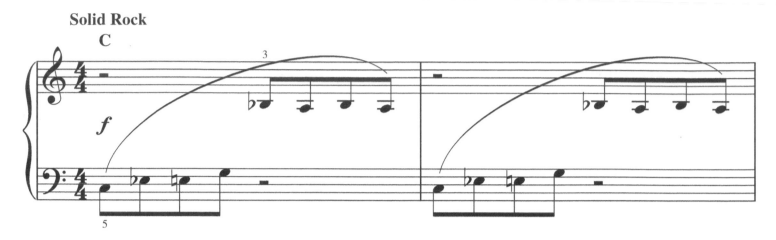

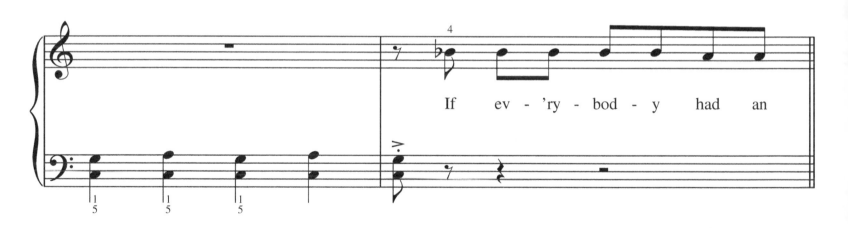

If ev - 'ry - bod - y had an

o - cean ___   a - cross the U. S. A. ___
route ___   we're gon - na take real soon. ___

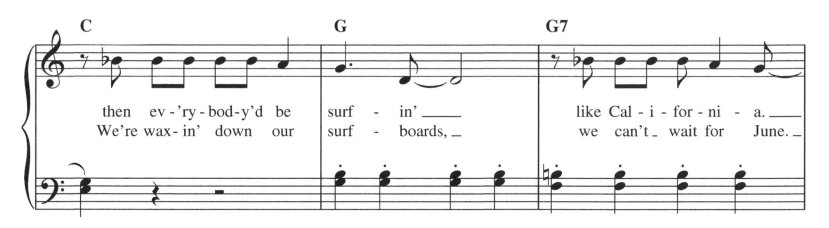

then ev-'ry-bod-y'd be surf - in' _____ like Cal-i-for-ni - a. ___
We're wax-in' down our surf - boards, _ we can't _ wait for June. _

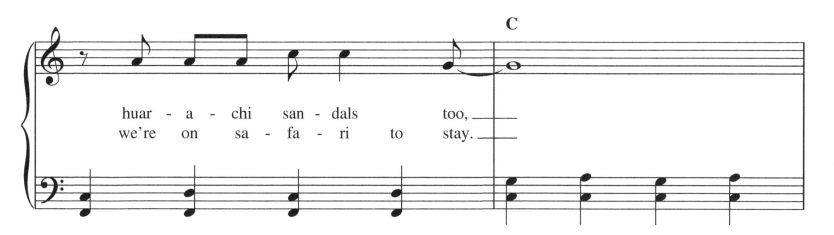

_ You'd see them wear-in' their bag - gies, _
_ We'll all be gone for the sum - mer, _

huar - a - chi san - dals too, ___
we're on sa - fa - ri to stay. _

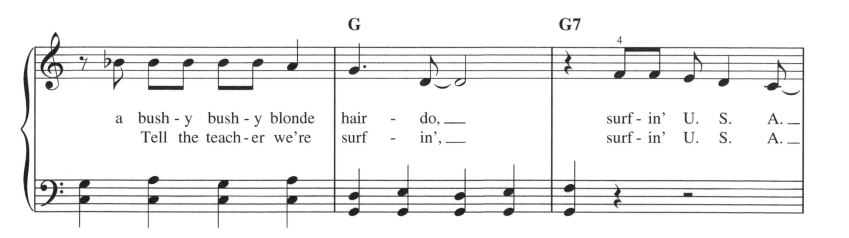

a bush-y bush-y blonde hair - do, _ surf-in' U. S. A. _
Tell the teach-er we're surf - in', _ surf-in' U. S. A. _

56

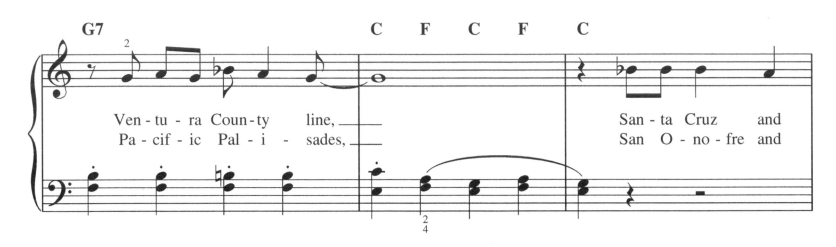

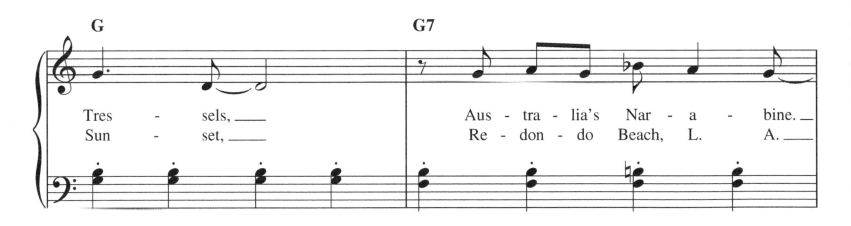

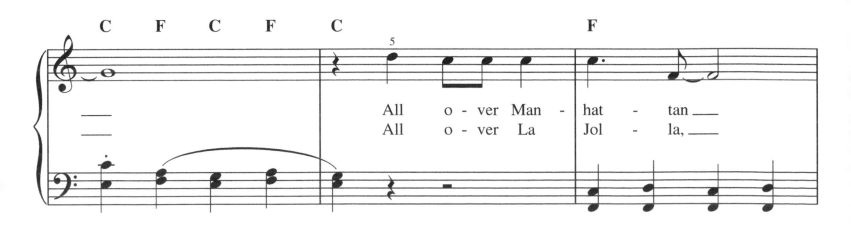

TWILIGHT TIME

Lyric by BUCK RAM
Music by MORTY NEVINS and AL NEVINS
Arranged by Phillip Keveren

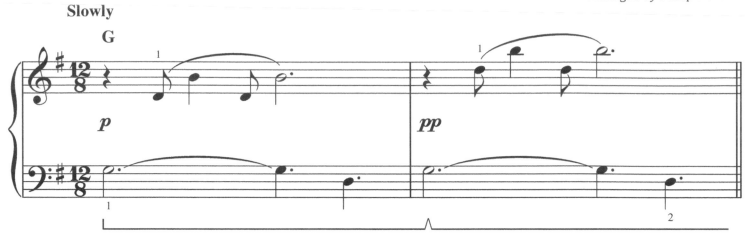

Heav-en-ly shades of night are fall-ing, it's twi-light time.
Deep-en-ing shad-ows gath-er splen-dor as day is done.

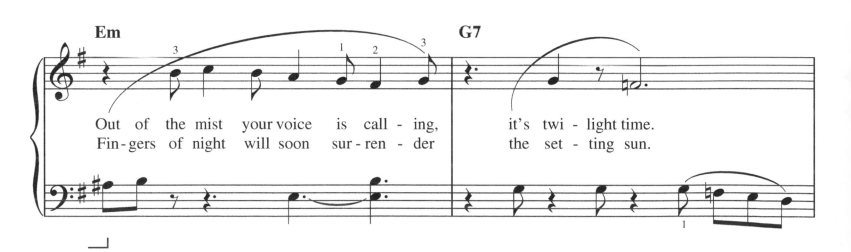

Out of the mist your voice is call-ing, it's twi-light time.
Fin-gers of night will soon sur-ren-der the set-ting sun.

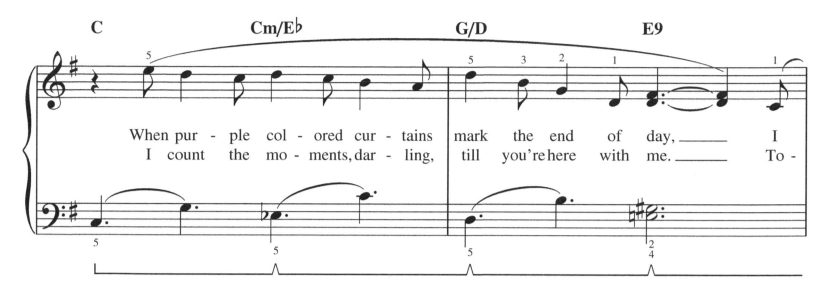

When pur - ple col - ored cur - tains   mark   the   end   of   day, _____   I
I   count   the   mo - ments, dar - ling,   till   you're here   with   me. _____   To -

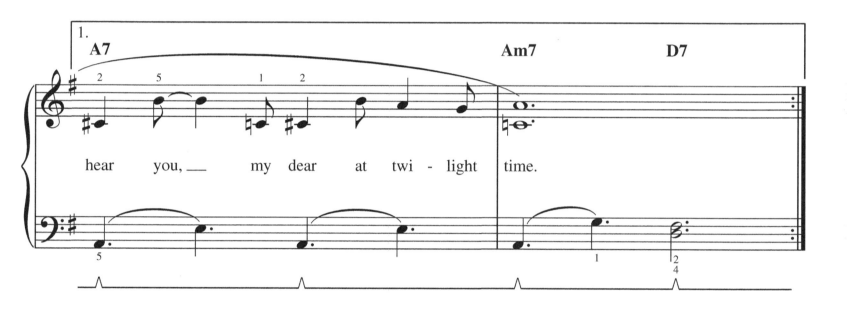

hear   you, ___   my   dear   at   twi - light   time.

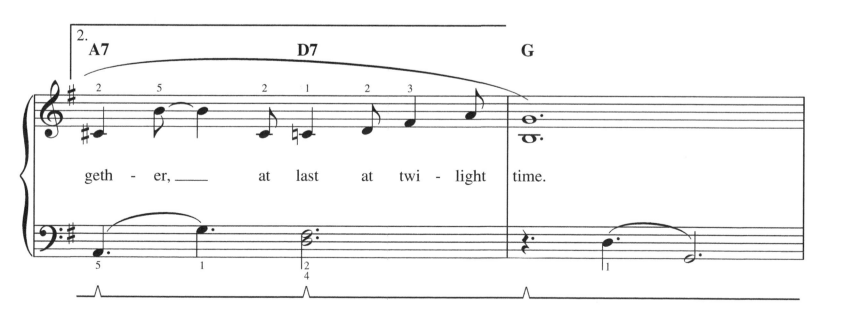

geth - er, _____   at   last   at   twi - light   time.

Here _____ in the af - ter-glow of day _____ we

keep our ren - dez - vous ___ be - neath the blue. ____

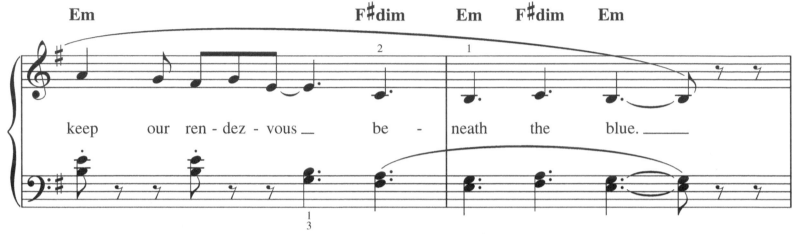

Here _____ in the sweet and same old way _____ I

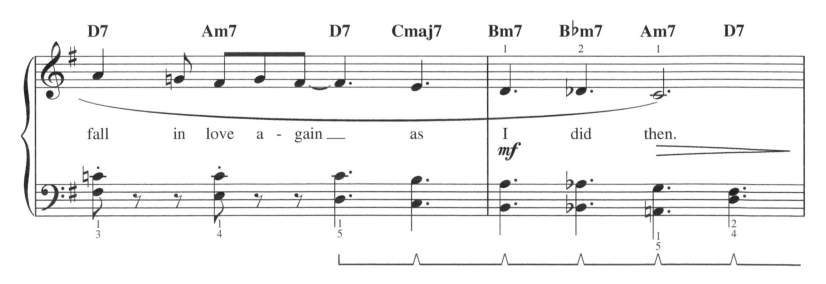

fall in love a - gain ___ as I did then.

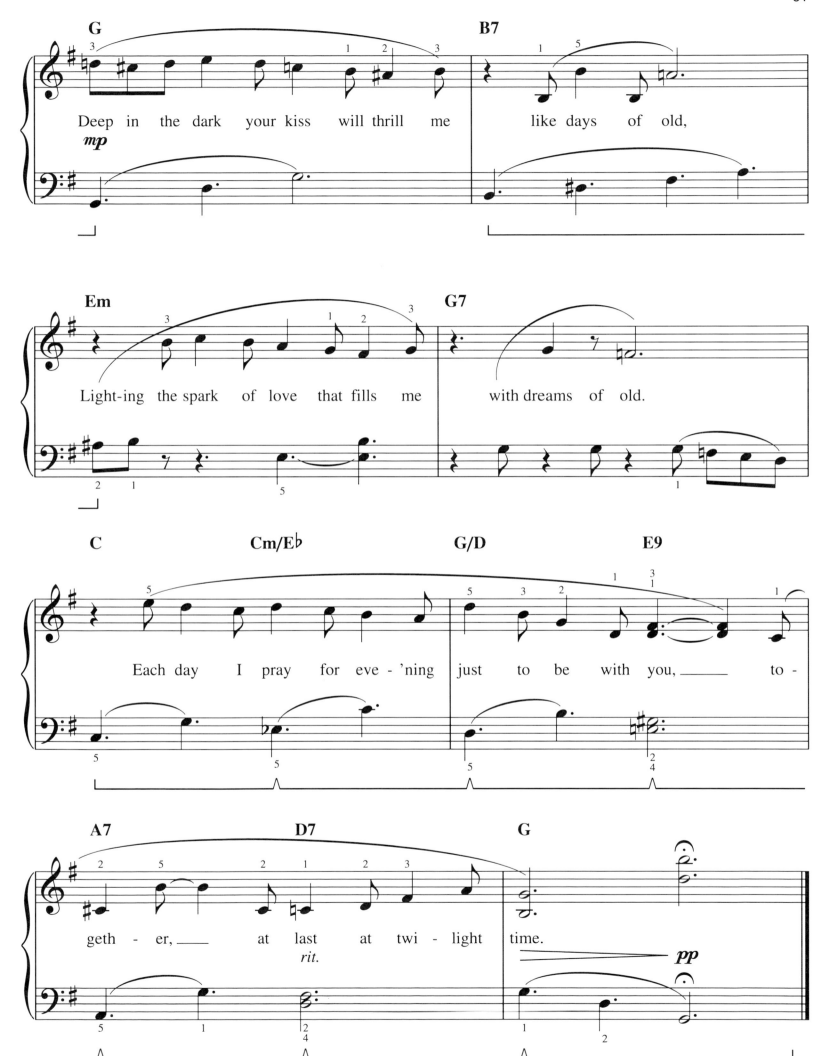

WILL YOU LOVE ME TOMORROW

(Will You Still Love Me Tomorrow)

Words and Music by GERRY GOFFIN
and CAROLE KING
Arranged by Phillip Keveren

Moderately slow

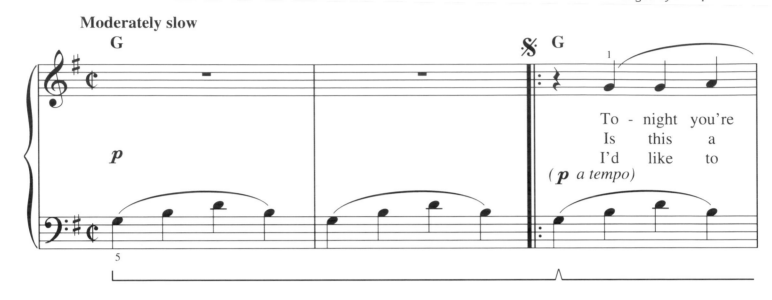

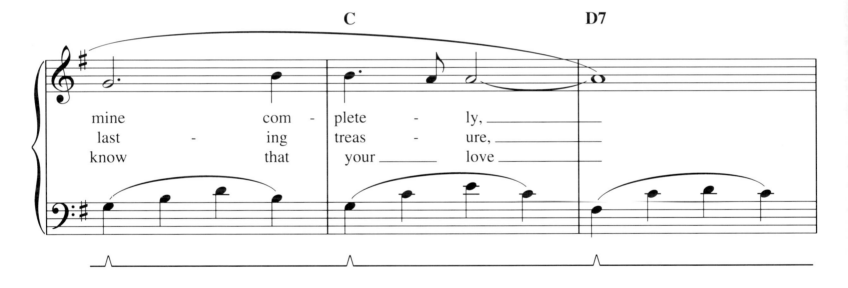

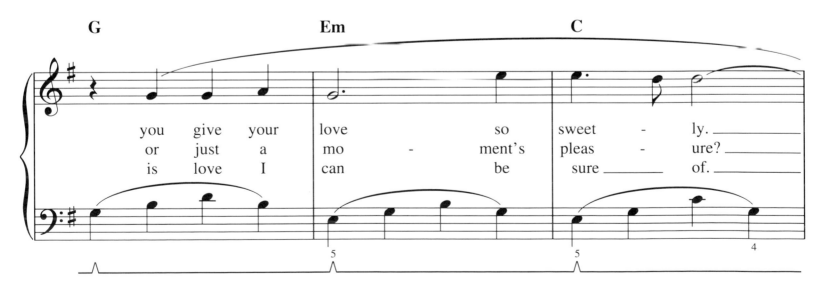

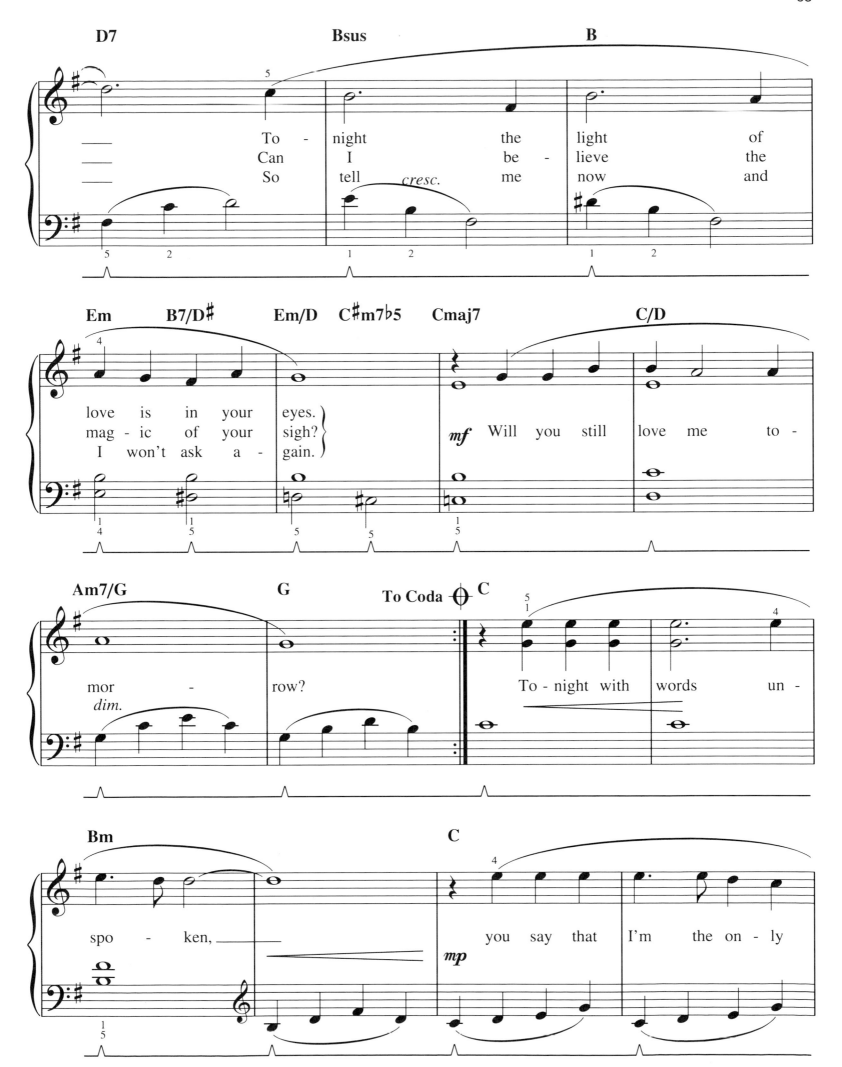

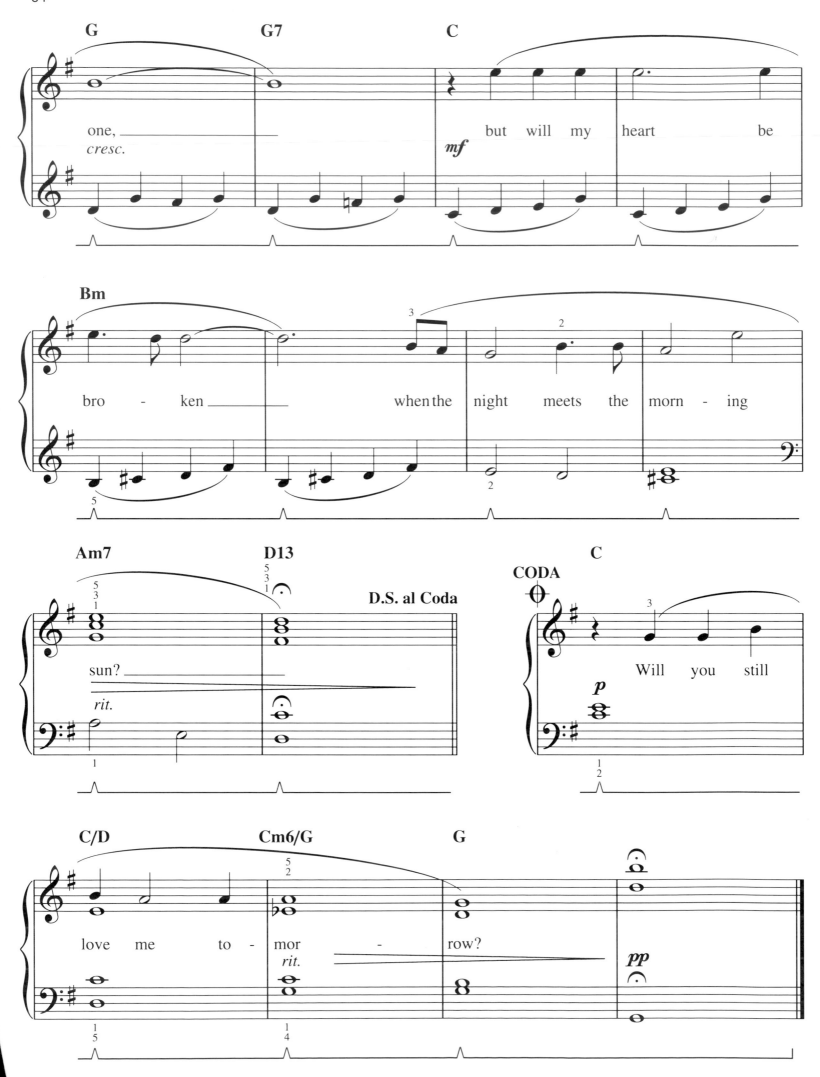